OCTOBER

OCTOBER

Carolyn Marie Souaid

NUAGE
EDITIONS

Cover design by Terry Gallagher/Doowah Design.
Photo of Carolyn Marie Souaid by Michel Gagnon.

Acknowledgements
Earlier versions of some of these poems have appeared in *The Antigonish Review* and *Prism International*.

This book was completed with the help of a grant from the Conseil des arts et des lettres du Québec. Many thanks to Karen Haughian and Gaston Bellemare and to my family for their continued support and encouragement. I am especially grateful to Michael Harris for his editorial eye, for his insight and friendship.

Excerpt from *Two Solitudes* reprinted with permission from Hugh MacLennan's estate, administered for McGill University by McGill-Queen's University Press.

We acknowledge the support of The Canada Council for the Arts and the Manitoba Arts Council for our publishing program.

Printed and bound in Canada by Veilleux Impression à Demande.

Canadian Cataloguing in Publication Data

Souaid, Carolyn Marie, 1959–
        October
Poems.
ISBN 0-921833-67-9

        1. Canada--English-French relations--Poetry.   I. Title.

PS8587.O87O38 1999   C811'.54   C99-901322-X
PR9199.3.S578O38 1999

Nuage Editions, P.O. Box 206, RPO Corydon, Winnipeg, Manitoba, R3M 3S7

for Michel

Two old races and religions meet here and live their separate legends, side by side. If this sprawling half-continent has a heart, here it is.
—Hugh MacLennan
Two Solitudes

CONTENTS

CHEZ NOUS

ARGUMENT

"...most people come to know only one corner of the room, one spot near the window, one narrow strip on which they keep walking back and forth."
—Rainer Maria Rilke

1

my mother taught us things
like birdtalk and how to blow bubbles
through soapy rings

taught us Latin words for flowers
and rhymes to wake up the trees

we marched in perfect time with her, tapping
the crazed syllables with our feet—

*if you step on a crack
you'll break your mother's back*

—one kid on either side, swinging her thin white arms
until we tired her out, and

resting in the cool shade at the park
watching us belly down the slide

I wonder

did she believe in God even then
as the clouds began zeroing in on her? was she conscious
of the kind of legacy
she'd be leaving us with?

that life is nothing
if not arbitrary, that one wrong step
could literally do a person in

★

I understood the cancer:

a lone dark bug feeding
on the liver, the kidneys, the brain

soon, a whole sinister network of them
working on her, ruthlessly

deliberately ending

in a huge black shadow
sweeping through her body
like the sudden darkness a cloud makes
when it crosses the sun

★

we missed our usual outings to the market
the rosy displays of produce and the one-legged accordionist

we missed the gypsy girl mulling cider by the cheese shop
the clobbered rumps of meat, hooked
and dangling from the ceiling

we could always tell that summer was dying

by the kinds of apples farmers were hauling off their trucks
and how the colours outside always bloomed and sharpened
in their final hours
before greying-down for good

it was the first miracle we'd known—

that perfect moment of stasis
before the year turned
and let loose the rain

★

one day I found a strange woman
sleeping in the guest bed

and no sign of my mother
anywhere

somehow she had vanished
in the middle of the night

the way an earthworm slips into the raw dirt
silently, leaving nothing behind
but an empty corridor
of itself

★

one by one, the relatives came to stay with us
older Church-going aunts
with grown-up kids of their own

ladies who wore black dresses all the time, who
spent most of the day chopping onions
smaller and smaller, frying up
the bits in hot oil

our house began taking on a new smell
as though a different family lived here

and although my father came home for meals
he always just sat at the table like a ghost, never talking to us
never once looking up

the only connection we had to my mother, the only news
came through muffled talk in the next room
the words *hospital* and *cancer*
worming their way through keyholes and
under the drafty cracks of doors

like something harmful
that would spread and destroy us all

soon I felt my knees give way
and parts of my body fold underneath
as though I, too, were starting to disappear

*

she leaned against my father on the long, strenuous walk
up to the house

wearing a stylish new pantsuit
and a flowered turban around her head
like one of those actresses
on the cover of her magazines

women who always come back
looking different in every movie
though fundamentally they're the same person

her hair grew back, and
June thickened with shadflies

and I told her about the evangelist who'd healed my best friend
of arthritis, how one day she just threw down her crutches
without thinking and walked outside
into the blinding sun
the way Lazarus, heeding the gentle hand of Christ
pulled himself up like a tender flower
out of the dirt

★

my mother drew the cool morning air
into her lungs
letting the world enter her suddenly
completely

stepping out after breakfast
in her bare feet and robe,
she'd feed on every detail in her garden
every crisp shade in the yard

each breath driving her shoulders a little higher
as though she were aiming for a piece of heaven, too

and when finally she couldn't hold it in any longer
she would exhale everything at once
letting the great, raw miracle
sweep through her body

ε

how often you've told me the same story, *mon amour*—
how your mother sat patiently in her chair, waiting
to die

though she never let on

how she made it
through each grey afternoon
with a cigarette and a tough glass of scotch

and the restless goings-on
in her head

it's not so much about giving up, you say
but letting go

★

we are a couple now with a kid, and you are telling me
that I don't know what it is to suffer
you are telling me about years, no—decades
of factory smoke in your mother's lungs

you are talking about entire communities
of women like this

old, hacking women with blankets across their knees,
fingers in a loose crochet on their lap

rocking themselves on the verandah
while the freight trains go by

it's no way to live a life, you say
and I am this close to (believing) you

★

I push a handful of bulbs into the dirt
around your mother's grave, wondering
why it was she never believed
in the simple flowers

and why her mauve and yellow crocuses
never came up from one year to the next

before dying, she told me stories about
the good God-fearing Catholics she knew
stuffing rags and newsprint into the cracks
of their cramped coldwater flats

and about musty mattresses in cruciform by the stove
five or six babies fighting
to keep warm

she told me about her friend Thérèse buying a Butterick dress
at the dimestore while her bastard of a husband
ploughed and seeded her kid in their own home

J'en ai assez vu, she said
Y existe pas, Dieu

it's that easy for a mother to pass darkness onto her child

it's just that easy
for someone to give up

★

in the end, what can I possibly say
to change your mind?

when Death comes for you
as He came for every one of your ancestors
will you let Him take you the way
He took your uncle with the plain blue tuque

its drooping tassel like the beaten tail of a workhorse
hauling his burden of wood to the sugar lodge?

will you let yourself drift away from us
open-mouthed in your hospital bed
your rows of teeth like blighted cornfields?

just how long can you go on thinking this way, an eternity
in your lidded coffin, speechless
among the worms?

let me try to convince you
again

OCTOBER

On October 10, 1970, Quebec's Minister of Labour, Pierre Laporte, was kidnapped outside of his St. Lambert home by the Chenier cell of a terrorist group known as the Front de Libération du Québec.

One week later, he was found dead in the trunk of a car...

SUMMER

(1969)

Someone tore the days off the calendar,
left our bodies groping
for the increments of time—

sun, moon, sun again,
moon.

The changing intensity
of light on water.

At dusk, we gathered
at the lip of the lake
with cigarettes and
a sexy paperback.

Spied on my aunt
drifting nude
in her rowboat

swimsuit hung like trout
over the side

wild birds' nest
of hair between
her legs.

In the mossy dark
the boys grew
strange appendages.

Sometimes, they came
to visit us in our
wooden bunks.

Then, as if the planets had conspired
against us, our world flew
out of whack—

I got my period.
A cousin walked clear through
a plate glass window. Another went mad
with poison oak

and one day on TV, an astronaut
sank his powerful toe
into the pimpled face
of the moon.

BAD LOT

Mum says we're not to play with the Doles who are a bad lot
but for some kid reason, I'm curious
their adopted daughter's a Cree Indian; her big brother
gags little girls and bullies them in the basement
when his mother is out. They get to eat weiners and fries
every day for lunch.

Mister calls me *Stinker*. Hollers it up and down the street
like an axe-murderer. He calls the French the *goddam French*.

It's pouring outside, everything blurring
like watercolour. Even in the dark I can see
the mother's cherry lips mouthing something shiny
through her Buick window—
Be a honey, kiddo, and save my 'do.
Then belting me in, *Don't you mind those crumbs back there*
and we rattle off to the train tracks to pick Mister Dole up from work.

Her lacquered fingernail shoos me out like a fly
while she sits at the wheel, jazzing up her hair.
Rain in my sneakers.
A slow black engine washing
into view.

Like a ghost, he is behind me,
tapping my shoulder,
a fine mist
of sweat on his face.

Suddenly, he is darting for the woods beyond the tracks,
splashing across the soggy field, he is shouting
sideways out of his mouth *I gotta take a whiz*
and I'm panting along behind
because he is a grown-up and I am a kid
and it is the only safe place to be.

We run for the tall trees until finally
they are closing in on us
like the dying summer days
and rain is sluicing off his chin
like his manic pee below.

He is muttering about the goddam French again,
flicking his thing around
like a huge, wet stallion airing himself dry.

Scumbags, he is saying.

All the way home
I can smell his splattered words
across my shoes.

WARNING

We bolted awake for Saturday cartoons,
roused by the dark, scraping hands of the clock,
huge pyjama cuffs dragging behind
as we tiptoed down to the basement,
thumbs hooked over our sloshing bowls of cereal.

Every week, we waited as the fluttering picture
stammered into focus, a giant American flag
rippling onscreen. When the music began,
we snapped to attention,
chirping through that anthem with heart
as though our teacher were lurking outside the house,
face pressed like a potato against the window,
eyeballs staring down on us from the raw dirt.

Like prayer time and "God Save the Queen" at school,
we had orders to follow
before the *Flintstones*—

that faceless man inside the television
whose booming voice always blew the giddy little hairs
straight up off my spine,
his air-raid message collapsing the walls around me
like the sudden wind in a house of cards.

This is a test of the emergency broadcast system, it said.
I repeat, this is only a test.

Then, clear off the spectrum, a high-end
h-o-o-o-o-o
ringing from the kitchen toaster coils.

Once, I thought Martians had landed in our yard.
A cool, blue dot seared the screen
long after I flicked off the set.

In that instant
I stopped breathing. I also stopped the earth
from coming apart.

MOVING ON

Our neighbours were a barometer of sorts,
their busywork signalling the end of summer—
Mister Dole sweeping down his walk, the rest
on ladders, scraping scaly old paint.
Brushing away the dead cells.

Night fell early.

We watched the houses darken,
our lonely porch lamp
as it flickered out,

tungsten's hot white tail
thinning into nothing.

This is how we measured change

cross-legged on the grass, fixed on the last lingering
strand of light—

the neighbour who lit himself on fire,
another who hung himself in the basement
with electrical cord, weighted body
like a grandfather pendulum, waving goodbye

goodbye.

THE LAST DAY

No one was safe anymore.

The Tremblay boys were on a rampage—
driving their bikes through people's gardens,
chloroforming innocent cats.
Their father'd run out on them.

We sought hideouts. Anywhere but home—
bins of hubcaps behind the strip mall,
a tree fort in the scrabby woods
which we decorated with dented boxes
and the skeletons of old chairs.

Everything came with us:
butterfly nets and Oreos,
our unwieldy wagon of dandelions
and popsicle sticks.

Venturing into the deepest
darkest leg of the forest, we stumbled
upon beer glass and a mud-licked Playboy
to smuggle back to the fort,
and as the sky began filling up with rain
I saw my father running toward us, a small man
in a grey windbreaker
and the terrifying black cloud
above him.

Red-faced, out of breath, he just shook his head
at the wooden studs nailed amateurishly
up the side of our tree
and said, nuzzling me like a sorry cub
into the booming hearth of his breast,
Someday, one of you kids is gonna get hurt.

OCTOBER

No one bothered to read
the signs—

agitated clouds, shattered
blue hydrangea

maples making dust
of their brilliant leaves,
making way

for snow

a housewife in taut light snapping
laundry from the line

frenetic birds
rushing the wind

★

6:15 p.m.

dark, whiskered men
paw the road
like mean-spirited dobermans

ears pricked, eyewhites
stark and jittering

moments before dinner,
not a breath in the house

apples in a dead mull
on the stove

★

6:17 p.m.

an old grey squirrel lugs his tail
across a high tension wire

one exhausted puff after the other

the doddering light
growing dim and unreliable
around him

★

Shadows drift through the house
silently, as rooms open into rooms,
a slow migration of darkness
along the floor

our faces grow monstrous
in the den, wattage down to one lamp
and the flickering blue eye
of television

like that night the Beatles played Ed Sullivan—

four grayish guys on our snowy Zenith,
shrill acoustics fighting the kitchen hum
of appliances, my mother's knitting hands
making electricity.

THE KIDNAPPING OF PIERRE LAPORTE

Mum said that when God closes a door
He opens a window someplace else.
This, after the neighbour's house
burnt down:

our mouths gaped at the sheer magnitude—
huge licking flames; the angry blast
of heat;

soon, just the ashen splinters of roof
and a man running, empty-handed
into the darkness.

That fall, my kid sister was born
and the reds and fuchsias flooded back
through the terra cotta pots
into our geraniums.

Today marks five years,
and as the wee one snuffs out the candles
on her birthday cake, as she wrings and bottlenecks
the perfect heads of balloons,

today, as three chocolatey fingers
stray into the open wonder
of her mouth

the rest of us gather by moonlight
in our Deathwatch
for a blue Chevy and its marked man
on their reckless course
through the cool, dark suck
of night.

HALLOWEEN NIGHT

We've made it to the underpass
miffed at City Hall
for bungling Halloween

we're walking with
sleeping bags and some matches
a long time it seems

our shadows growing wayward
in the light

soon, an old pickup
putters by

its dirty wind
ruffling our hair

eases off the road, and
shuts down, waiting

the men's orangey faces
hazed in cigarette smoke, their filed
jack-o'-lantern teeth

then I'm not sure what comes next
the baritone darkness between the driver's legs
or my friend, pattering for the ditch
like a startled fawn

but a curious tightening in my calves
keeps me pinned there, momentarily
while the man on the passenger side
slowly leans out the window,
hands starting up like bats
in the night

later, I catch up with my friend
crouched in the woods
button eyes blinking
through a thin mask
of leaves

trembling, we roll our sleeping bags
along the cold, bearded ground

moon looking straight through us
like the Evil Eye, like God
like my mother, white-lipped
in her kitchen chair

levelling me
with silence.

HERCULES
(The War Measures Act)

The tanks are rolling into Montreal.

Meanwhile, in our small suburb across the river
we are minutes from showtime,

steadying blowaway props on the driveway
for our first and only performance of *Hercules*.
Among the garageful of spectators—Mister Dole
tucked nervously between a canoe and the garden tools, an ear
to the whispering radio in his palm;
Eddy Shaughnessy with a pail on his head
hollering *When do we get to kiss the cyclops?*

The crazy pages of the script have come loose
and are flying about the yard.

Last week in a movie, battalions
of ominous birds beaked down on a city
while the innocents ran helplessly for cover.
And these items on the news: a professor
jailed for hiding a dangerous book in his coat;
the SWAT team ripping through a wall
to cuff an infamous *femme fatale*. The camera zoomed in
on the yellow, winged light as they dragged her out,
her heavy, saucer lids.

A chopper bullets dangerously close,
sends rippled air
muscling over the neighbourhood.

The clouds in the sky are moving fast.

We gather onstage—gods, centaurs, monsters.
Like a foolish wrestler, my eight-year-old brother
thunders onto the scene in his underwear,
bunching his tiny hand
into the meanest fist he can.

LAST THOUGHTS OF PIERRE LAPORTE, STUFFED AND LEFT IN A CAR TRUNK AT ST. HUBERT AIRBASE

Their jackal eyes, their cool
upturned collars

the holy chain on my neck, my wife, my kids
my lamp-lit bungalow

downtown drunks and their pointless lives
like beads of a broken rosary
pinging across the floor

Domtar men with heart conditions, midnight jobs
stirring soupy vats of paper

forebears on the stony land
ragged, broken men

livestock bred into madness

the world tipped on its side
unstoppable, the whirring
in my brain

the suffocating darkness

just wanting a pillow
and a last grab of air.

AFTER THE FIRST DEATH

When someone dies, all you can do
is lie in bed
like a worm of toothpaste, wincing
at the clinical starch of day—

grating sunlight on the walls, metallic
voices on the radio.

He's in the dark drawer, eyes frosted shut.
Body like a cold potato in the ground.

You know it will always be this way.

One man dead. Another—your uncle—
on his way out. Eyewhites yellowing
in the hospital bed.

All of a sudden, your mother's meat loaf
will stop tasting right
and Sundays will leave you
saddened at the wilting vine
on an autumn fence or the absent sun
like a dead piano key.

Dead, no matter how hard you bang it.

MORTALITY

Every sound, every small vibration
is a lesson from God, a reminder
of our own slim time
on earth

utterings of the sudden beginnings
and endings of things—

radio voices rising and falling
over the airwaves

a hairbrush
slipping from my mother's grasp

the firecracker static
of socks on a dry rug

her quivering hand
on the doorknob

the words *We have to tell the children*

my heart starting up
like a thousand soldiers
drumming off to war

our neighbour's mean yellow dog
roughing up a garbage can

Dad's restless weight
on the bedspring

the house quietly draining
of light.

THURSDAY NIGHT

Days after the murder: we were driving
home from Brownies, stars all jumbled up in the sky
when it happened—Mister Shaughnessy went ballistic on me
for speaking French to Nathalie who didn't know
a word of English.

Everybody speaks White in this car! he snapped
and all of us just sat there, trembling
in the divided air,

small of our backs
stapled against the cold vinyl.

My mind reeled: What brother turned on a brother?
How depraved did you have to be
to actually kill someone
with your bare hands?

For a split second, there was a frightening imbalance
in the air, then he simply lost control
of the wheel. I felt the blood drain
from me as we roared up the sidewalk
and then I heard the body of the car crumple
like a piece of cardboard.

He jammed on the brakes.

I thought of lunging at him, my pronged ring
leaving viperous dots of blood on his cheek,
I thought of a cold knife pressed against the base
of his throat, I thought of its starry blade
making a quick fish-slit, I thought unflinchingly
of everything.

I waited a moment, and then the huge animal
inside me
fell silent.

POST-MORTEM

(Prince Edward Island, 1970)

Beach blackened with seaweed.
Beyond—the steady surf, wind
rolling backwards on waves.

Repetitive days

scabbed with clouds
and gulls veering low
over water.

A man in slippers
outside his clapboard house
wonders why
the barbecue won't start up.

A plane ride away
little has changed
despite news of a man's death
in Quebec.

ESCAPE

In the recurring dream, I am locked
in my cupboard under the sink,
hot-water pipes leaving twin burns
along my wrists.

I am headed
nowhere

like the snaking line
of the damned

inching
decimal by decimal
into oblivion

or the murdered man
bumping around in a car trunk,
feet blundering
north, south, east, west
like the fibrillating compass
of his head.

In the dream, my hands are tied
while the killers go free

memorizing a trap door
in the horizon

popping the padlock and reappearing
unmanacled, to the bright nod of camera lights,
to flares along the runway
and their brilliant getaway
planes.

ROAD TO TORONTO
(Spring Break)

Everyone's tired of Quebec
in March—houses chained
with ice,

orchards creaking under the weight
of snow.

My father warms the car.
We strap on suitcases, bikes.

Our cat yawns and settles, moonshaped
into the window sill. Fading
from the devastated street,

the frenetic footprints
out of town.

His marble eye holds us
until we dissolve into the horizon,
mewing points of light
in the blank and isolate space
of his brain.

Somewhere, on the other side
we re-enter the atmosphere, burning
through the glaze of spring and
the new green woods

raw burst of light and chrome
along the galloping highway.

GENS DU PAYS

QUEEN ELIZABETH

At five, I was queen
in the school pageant, spent weeks
prancing around the house in a tinfoil crown,
eager to perform, until Opening Night
when I grasped the enormity
of the thing,

the whitened panic of the crowd,
the live, breathing darkness

floodlights like the glaring eyes of God
as boy after boy kissed my hand, miniature Mounties
barely out of diapers, their small glazed faces
pressing into Mum's diamond ring

backing me accidentally into a prop,
a wobbling mural of orphans
kneeling in the drought,
their upcast eyes
wet with hope.

Imagine it—a scrawny kid in Cinderella sleeves,
the whole teetering world on her shoulders.

GENERAL JAMES WOLFE

According to history, you slumped to the ground
in a scarlet cape, heart buffaloed by the cannons,
blackened blood sieving from an open wound,

your final gag of air viewed by two nobodies
and the damp, heavy-scented pines.

Yesterday, you came to me in a dream—
chinless kid factoring equations on the blackboard,
eyeglasses and fish-white legs drawing classroom laughs
while the dogged machinery of your brain
lay awake nights, plotting
the ultimate parabola
of revenge.

In the 1770 painting, you are a different dying man,
face tipped back, soulful body opened like a prayerbook
to the angels. Aesthetically, it is a pleasing fiction—

sun poking through the conifers,
eleven mourners at your feet.

Death seeping into your bones
like warm water.

TADPOLES

We fished them out of the pond
one by one, the babies even

laying them on their glossy backs,
flat belly-whites flashing in the heat.
It was all premeditated, a recess prank
over root beer and chips. We'd whittled our sticks
into spears, it would be easy as ripping into chicken,
our serrated supper-knives glinting.

I went first, it meant nothing to me,
watching it jerk and quiver in the grass
like a bare nerve
while the other kids stood wide-eyed
on the muddy bank, slender bodies wavering
in the green water.

After that, we bludgeoned them one by one,
howling at the splat of their jelly centres
through the startled lining
of their mouths.

Howling.

We should have *wept.*

ÉMILE NELLIGAN

Your picture was a gift item in tourist shops on The Main—
keepsake for poets and dreamers
toiling in obscurity, and then
suddenly, you were a mania
of bookmarks and puzzles all over the city,
a brooding darkness
xeroxed so many times
your face turned white as a ghost.

Legend has it your parents drove you to madness:
Maman and an Irish father
drawing battle lines
down the gentle plane of your skull,
poisoning the world inside you
until all that remained was your lunatic shell—
tightrope for a smile, irises dead in their whites
having already fled to a greener place.

Rimbaud, Baudelaire, you followed them all
into the rose café, praising the crystalline air
and the drunken rush of spring.

You, your own mighty metaphor
against the whitening sky.

MY FATHER

Here's the thing: we weren't rich. Like his old man,
my father just knew how to stretch a buck, nagged us hourly
about the cost of electricity and long-distance calls
so that Sundays, he could blow the bundle on us
at Ruby Foo's Restaurant
with Uncle Raymond and the gang.

Nothing like a pupu platter and a good cigar, he'd say
having bitten the road all week
with his suitcase of bargains.

Parting the glass doors, he'd grin
like a man who's struck a deal on shoes for the kids
and we'd clamor in under his frayed sleeve,
bold as bubblegum.

Mum, in Easter-best, would pause a moment in the lobby
to straighten her hatpin, or drag a bright nub of lipstick
around her mouth before shooing us
through the crimson room of tailored men and mobster types
clinking glasses of liquor and ice,

their polished wives
on tufted chairs,
glittering.

Starstruck, she'd bend my ear like a school girl—
Look, it's a Bronfman!
or *There's Daniel Johnson, over there.*
Now that man was one of the good ones
you ask your father.

By mid-afternoon, our table degenerated—
egg rolls lolling in plum sauce,
Raymond with the coat-check girl,
talking up the hockey game.
Dad nodding off with a cigar in his mouth,
tie askew,
a kind of fallen angel,

life piling up around him
like bills in his pocket,
the yard goods, the road trips, the no-name towns he stomachs
for this—his hard-earned swatch
of heaven.

MON ONCLE RICHARD

Mon Oncle Richard died last night though no one in the family
gives a good goddam: he'd always been hankering
to be someplace else.

Saturdays at Ti-Oui's he sat with the other guys,
slumped on a stool by the juice machine, eyeballs longing
after the drunken swim of Tang.
Walk in any time and you'd find him there,
cauliflower cross-section of his brain working overtime
with his crudded fingernail to scratch a loto-card.
Give him Jacques Cartier Bridge and he'd have been the first
to dive into the nasty waters
of the St. Lawrence.

He was a mean bugger. The way he sat at the bar all night
humming *Johnny B. Goode* while his only daughter was getting married
in the next room. Or that year during the *réveillon* meal
when he jabbed a fork into the *tourtière* and told his saint of a wife
in front of everyone he'd rather be taking abuse on the job
than choke *that* down his throat.
Crisse de ciment, he barked. *Crisse de Noël.*

Now that the little guy's gone, I feel ten pounds lighter
knowing that the Angel of Darkness has finally jumped ship
and is out there in the middle of nowhere, fighting
his miserable way across the current.

PORTRAIT OF A TERRORIST

Do you remember the things you saw as a child?
Backyards of beer cans and auto parts,
kids darting through the sprinkler
on a morsel of lawn.

Steam rising from the tub where you soaked
in your muzzy bathwater fart, pale boy
clutching the thin motel soap
your mother brought back
from Wildwood one year—

the cleanest thing you'd ever smelled.

A hot dog joint rubbing up against
a nunnery.

Your mother's wire brassière
looped over a doorknob and her brash sunset
of makeup on the pillow.

The coiled black fire escape
where you crouched with a thin book of poems
until you made a pact with the gods
and the wind of garbage-smell and roses
finally carried you away.

LA GROSSE MAUDITE ANGLAISE

For a third time, the same sluggard goes to relieve himself
at the back of the bus. Everyone braces himself
for another view of the skintight bowling shirt,
the crude bumblings up the aisle
as he shifts his drunken weight through the bus,
bumping every elbow along the way.

One by one, we turn away from him
focusing, reluctantly, on the passing scenery—

the anemic horizon and its lowly tractor
rusting in a field

a motley contingent of goats
and other eyesores.

Later that night, you take me to see *Octobre* by Pierre Falardeau
and we make it in just as the theatre darkens
like an eyelid over the world.

In the first scene, the actors are way out of focus
but as my eyes adjust to the white, muscled flicker of the screen
it turns out that the villains are actually heroes
who live near abattoirs and electrical transformers,
guys who say things like *On est fait comme des rats*
and *le gouvernement est une maudite grosse machine*

guys who read Gaston Miron and eat beans out of a can,
guys who own nothing
but a couple of decomposed vegetables in the fridge.

In one scene they're escaping with the prisoner
they're going to murder, they are inching
past the dumb cops, they are almost home free
and the feathered hairs along the nape of my neck
are literally rising in anticipation.

But when the lights come on
my face is hot with tears and all the French kids
are upright on their plush chairs, whooping and clapping
for the scruffy thug who snuffed a man because of Westmount,
because of pond-scum drinking water, because someone had to pay
for swiping the crumb from his brother's mouth,
and I find myself annoyed at the lot of them,
just plain pissed off
at the mentality.

Forget the movies.

Let's just say we are all passengers on the same bus
only this time, I'm the odd man out

the loathsome traveller tottering up the aisle,
la grosse maudite anglaise
knocking them one by one
as I go.

FORTUNE

A squeegee kid with blue hair and
calluses on the bare soles
of her feet

shoves pretzels and Coke
into her mouth.

Her shell-shocked face
a war zone of pimples and
nose rings.

Beside her, purring
on the sidewalk, her baby
in a Sunkist box

hungry and smaller than
my cat.

POEM FOR NATHALIE AND HER ANGLO HUSBAND

There's a hole in the ozone the size of Sorel
but you go on—small humming body—clinging to your world,
kinship of mothers around a coffeepot, oblivious
to the insects in your own yard,
their desperate renovations.

Sundown, and your warm dog on linoleum.
You, sipping sherry. Blunt-headed bugs
whacking the porch screen.

Your gaze drifts up over the bubble of children
and your husband grilling sirloin. You should be paring potatoes
but, instead, you're contemplating a hot dog you ate last March,
the shape your life took with a rumpled boyfriend
spraypainting *Oui*
through the back lanes of St. Denis

the mere mention of aluminum siding
or an obedient vine of clematis
and you would have died.

The new you is a stretch, a leap in faith
for your kids, for your clothes
summering in mothballs, for the poetry
you've discovered in a lopsided banana loaf
or your gold, filigreed patterns of china.

The new you, desperately, vehemently
reaching.

IMMIGRANT

1

He touches up walls for a living,
masking and buffing imperfections,
probing their rhythms
the way a blind man presses his ear to the world,

the rhythm of his own life a little off—
bankruptcy, a brother's murder,

midnight runs to the drugstore for his fragile wife,
wallowing on the bed and weeping
for her devastated womb.

Mornings tinged with exhaust
he pencils his way along the avenue,
black bread and coffee beans
in an honest paper bag.

Every week, a new job, shimmering terraces
of paint in a tray,

his leaden eyes skirting
the customer—college girl, sexpot—
someone he might have had
in another life.

Sometimes while he works, he feels
the tremor of children
in her walls.

2

His parents fled the homeland at night,
two stick figures with their slim bag
of possessions, youthful

and stuffed with hope, sailing for
a glimmer of light
on the horizon—

a brushstroke of land
and their unborn children,
huddled like treasures
in the rich, red pigment
of the soil.

3

His hands are swollen from overtime
split and imperfect,
cuneiform dirt moons
where the nails have broken free
of their fingertips

—small, downturned mouths.

In Spain, they might've been Picasso's hands;
in Amsterdam, Rembrandt's

letting go of the grandfather trunk
and the furniture on his back

bursting up the scaffold with oils and glazes,
jump-starting the canvas like a tormented soul
roaming the world, overtaken
by his final destination—

a most ornate and dazzling cathedral,
its mammoth shadow consuming him
like a guttural sob
from the darkest room of his heart.

ORPHAN

1

We rescued you from Lebanon
in a covered bassinet, bedsheets sewn
into perfect white sails
over your head,

infant orphan
whizzing across time zones
to our sunny coastline
on the edge of the world,

modern tea-and-spice explorer
rerouted by Fate

into the glorious blue mouth
of the St. Lawrence.

2

Tadoussac: Your Dad and I on a bald rock,
peering through binoculars. Perfect, nectarine light.

Watermelon reflections
of yachts in the harbour

and you, a speck on the beach
shovelling sand into your bright pail.

Suddenly, a gust of motorcycles along the boardwalk:
men and their beer-bottle tans,

hot, white sun muscling
down their backs.

Clearly, it frightens you—this monstrous sighting
of blackflies on the horizon,

your crazed toes leaving bird tracks behind.

The sailor's cap blown off your head, a seagull
against the darkening sky.

Later, flattened against a pillow, you scream
from the motel cot,
the dream gripping you
in waves:

your sea-drenched body at the prow of a ship
negotiating a squall, your overturned vessel
caught in the toilet flush of two rivers

hellbound.

3

I cannot trust you to make your own way
in this world, the way I once ran beside you
holding your bike and suddenly let go
giving you a good fifteen seconds
of pure, exhilarating flight.
Wordlessly I stood there
as you headed for a blip in the asphalt
handlebars overtaking you, fenders caught
in the butterflying sunlight.

You could say I just want to save you
from the push and pull
of politics.

The New World is rusted with Coke cans. So are the parks.
You've had to learn about AIDS and school shootings
and how to recognize a used syringe. I've had to explain
the difference between *joual* and CBC French, that *poutine*
and trailer parks and men in Speedo bathing suits are *kétaine*.

On TV, separatists are burning the Canadian flag.

You came to us wide-eyed and innocent
and all I want is to keep you
safe.

CHEZ NOUS

JE ME SOUVIENS

You say *necessary, but unjustifiable.*
I call it *murder,* plain as day.

It's like walking down the street together
but being in two different afternoons.

Long ago, at the Santa Parade, you clung
piggy-backed to your father,
gazing smack into the world he saw—broken streets
thinly veiled as Christmas. Kids from the orphanage
pawing Ogilvy's window, elves in warm plaids
winking and waving at them from a conveyor belt.

A nobody on the corner, begging for a dime
gloves bitten off at the thumbs.

Though we haven't crossed paths yet—won't for 20 years—
I'm in that holiday store with my mother
shopping for patent leather shoes.
A string is looped around my finger.
Floating at the end of it,
a lazy red balloon.

Outside in the scant light, your dad grips your ankles tightly.
Warns you to pay attention, never to let go.

The twinkling snowflakes in his hair
are brighter than the stars.

VERSIONS OF A STORY

My uncle feeds us stories about growing up
during the Depression,
how his schoolmates used to eyeball him at recess
while he polished off a tart red apple,

how they'd wait patiently for him
to take that last succulent bite
before tossing it over his shoulder.

How they'd all lunge like scavengers
for his thin scraps.

Playing out, it is pure theatre of the absurd—
the masticated fruit in its snail-paced trajectory
down the throat,

their drooling mouths like overfilled glasses
gushing at the rim,

eyes opened wide as quarters
before the vulturous climax
at the core.

I tell you, he says. *Whoever got his hands on that thing*
was a damn lucky bastard.

It's just this side of slapstick.

Your Matante Ginette tells the same story
with a different cast of characters.

The "lunging" in it
verging on melodrama.

In it, a fat English boss is at the window
gazing several storeys down. He is on the phone
and stubbing his cigar into the open palm
of an ashtray—

*Shit, I'll just hire the next guy in line
my dog barks at.*

Down below, a dozen of your relatives are lapping at
the huge gates of an asbestos mine,
their fibrous 5 a.m. lungs
like steel wool.

THE OLD DAYS

The older guys filled your ears with it
when you were a summer kid earning cash at the mill.
Stories of Montreal in the forties,
ivied mansions at one end of town, sweatshops
at the other, a mum green mountain
wedging them apart.

Aldérie had one about a big-breasted French girl
in the backseat of his buddy's cab
nuzzled into the finest English wool of a man's suit;
parting his trousers and entering them
with the candied glee of an orphan
roaming Eaton's toy department at Christmas,
a fistful of jingling dimes.

The thought made him sick—the guy's hard organ swelling
like a church bell on Sunday, the barest blue light
of dawn washing over them.

A pig like that with a little girl, he said.
Comme ta p'tite soeur à toé, ou la mienne.

All through your shift, you pictured the rest—
the driver's pupils floating in the rear view mirror, helpless
as the day his kid sister drowned in the Saguenay,
so preoccupied he doesn't even notice
the passing store windows
of First Communion dresses and little-boy skates,

the bald short-order cook
peeing against a brick wall.

Somehow, you knew how it would all end—
the girl getting tossed out like garbage
by the side of the road, mouth smudged,
convent tunic tussling with the wind;

the driver pocketing a coin or two,
vanishing into traffic
in mute, underwater silence.

OUTSIDE MY LOVER'S DORM ROOM
ON THE EVE OF THE REFERENDUM
(1980)

From your half-open door, I watch you
lift the fleur-de-lys
to your window, onto the impoverished skyline—
rambling scrapyard of buildings and rain.

There's a slight tension
in your thumb, the nervous rush of nylon as
you fumble with a crease

inexplicable, until I glimpse a second figure
in the shadows, slim line of her body
tottering on a ladder

blonde hair and freshman sweats
swaying toward you, arms outstretched

scene playing out
like the wavering finale
of a tossed coin.

REFERENDUM DAY IN CHARLEVOIX

A farmer with third-grade education
ploughs through the crowded gym for a turn
behind the black curtain. He wears a dark suit,
his only suit, the one he wears at weddings and funerals,
the stiff shirt collar
troubling his Adam's apple.

In the secret booth, he bends down
until his nose is two inches from the ballot,
steadying his good hand long enough
to plant a wobbling X in the rectangle
for his home, his children

for the eager saplings bordering the fence-line.

Released from duty, he loosens the top button,
dabs his misted head with a hankie and retraces his path
along the dirt road, one plodding foot after another
until the familiar bald top of his silo
reappears over the horizon.

Downwind in the big city, the news is bad—
rows of scarred tenements clouded in barbecue smoke,

les bons vivants flaked out in undershirts
on their balconies, listening to the pigeons
slap around the garbage cans.

Soon, something bigger than the moon
creeps into the meager twilight—
bitterness, loss, regret.

Regardless

the farmer rises at five every morning,
throws a hoe over his shoulder
and drops one more seed
into the grateful soil.

THE DANCE

Now that you've both left, I'm alone in the kitchen
with my teacup and the paper
and leftovers of the morning rush—

Lego fanned across the den, Alex's pyjamas
pooled on the floor by the television
like a caterpillar's rumpled skin, your dishes
of small gritty boulders,
bacon fat hardening
on the window sill.

Already, there's no stopping it—each clumsy hop of the second hand
adds mileage between us and another day
of stuff.

The sun's slid down the fridge like sherbet, has reappeared
as two glum oblongs on the linoleum, while for you
I'll bet, it's pancaked across your windshield.
A flashy, white thing you need sunglasses for
just so you can tolerate vision.

I'll bet the top's down, your hair blown straight back off your face,
I'll bet you're fiddling for a decent radio station,
bypassing everything English along the way
including the oncoming STOP sign
whose linguistic viability hasn't been ruled on
though it's still a perfectly good verb in France.

In case you're interested, my tea's down to the cold dregs
and I'm reading stuff in the paper—
17,436   8,947   10,420   11,325
8,642   7,618   4,129.
Quebecers coming, Quebecers going. By the planeload.

I'm doodling a bunch of happy faces on my napkin
and crossing them out. Already, I've answered the phone five times.

I do not want to carpool with the neighbour's kids.
I do not want to buy a Filter Queen.
I do not want a wallet made by an ex-con.
I do not need a subscription to *Le Devoir*
        to make me an enlightened anglo
in Quebec. I do not need a subscription to *The Gazette*
        to make me an enlightened anglo in Quebec.

If you really want to know, the sun's soft-shoed its way
to the middle of the floor and somehow
the two disparate shapes have fused into a parallelogram of sorts.
My left shoulder is brushing up against
a note you taped to the wall, stuff our son has to know
for Friday's test: 35 spelling words.

The first one is *la danse.*

ON THE EVE OF ALL SAINTS'

Ghosts in the cellar, festering in the dark.
Stirring up trouble the way, outside, under the hooked trees
little neighbours in Halloween masks
bicker over loot bags—

Maurice Duplessis, René Levesque, Robert Bourassa,
Félix Leclerc, Lionel Groulx, Pierre Vallières,
Pierre Laporte.

Tonight, again, you blamed me for history.

For the Plains of Abraham
and "traitors" hung by their scrawny necks,
for the Queen and the fat Jew slumlords,

for the gaping crack in our wall,
black and barbed
as a spider leg.

Your long face took you to a barstool
and glared back at you
from a chilled stein of beer—

rippling skull and crossbones,

the rest of us drifting at the periphery—
our son, your untouched half of the bed,
the cantankerous hot-water pipes.

SUNDAY DRIVE

And if this were the last day,
what would be remembered
of our time on earth?
What triviality
would we have ended on?

The white peaked tent
in Carré St. Louis. Children with their
carnival faces, cartwheeling through the grass.
Our overheated car
fighting to park.

Our boy in the back seat,
verging on sunstroke.

Not a Bengal tiger, nor a postmodern painting
but the flowers outside his window.

Their brazen stripes
bringing him a sudden wave of nausea.
Petals wilting in the humidity.

Our life on earth.
Before the apocalypse,
the asteroid, the final eruption
of Mount Royal:

Hey! Let's go to Ottawa to see the tulips!

Maudite bonne idée.
En même temps
on ira voir les légumes
au parlement.

MOMENT

After our fight in the kitchen,
you couldn't touch me in bed
and all I could think about was that evening
downtown when we stood, dumbfounded
under the tittering stars, police chalk-line of a body
between us, your unbearable silence
as the ambulance petered out, cold
dead heap of a man wailing into the distance.

The way you just stood there on the sidewalk
clutching your black umbrella
though it never rained.

SIX-YEAR-OLD

Alex is home today, pale with flu
vows he'll never play with some kid at school—

His skin. It's so-o-o black, he says.

There's no bite in his voice, just plain fact, the way he refuses
an afternoon haircut or the spinach on his plate, hand held up
like a cop directing traffic. The conversation is over now, he is busy
bulldozing his playdough, working the plump heel of his hand
into the tough blue lump—pounding it, slapping it.
Impulsively, I want to turn him upside down, shake him
with the whole shocking history of the world,
the soft heap of bodies at Auschwitz and slaves
on their cotton plantations, my father-in-law
working double time at the paper mill
to put supper on the table.

But I am cold and silent, and his upper body is at a desperate angle
feeding clay through a metal sieve, stunned
at how he's made squid out of matter, how
with one touch of the hand he's able to destroy everything
that's whole.

ROADRUNNER AND COYOTE

Two empty wine glasses, the cat in his quiet corner
lapping up yesterday's meal—this is the cockeyed world
as you entered it

early this morning
when you crept downstairs with a blanket
and your ragamuffin toy.

Your Dad gunning out of the driveway.
Me, by the kitchen sink, waiting for daylight
to come crawling back.

This is the scene you passed up

for television and a few laughs, the ongoing spat
between Roadrunner and Coyote.

At your age, you've already decided that none of it is real—
the cartoon sky, the insubstantial poof Coyote makes
when he hits the ground

the boulder tailing him relentlessly off the cliff
gathering momentum, like a dark
freefalling storm cloud.

Somehow, you know that nothing

—especially not the flimsy cocktail parasol
he's holding over his head—

will save him.

SELF-PORTRAIT

Our boy hates kindergarten, this business of arts and crafts
of cramming a page with houses and trees

to quell some neurotic teacher's fear
of the void.

He draws a vaguely human head and keyboard teeth.
Straight through the forehead, an eye
like a fried egg.

A misshapen, armless thing, none the likes of you
or me.

As for sculpture, never mind.

In the end, of course, what does it matter,
given all he knows of dinosaurs and doom,
of one volatile asteroid,

his entire world
another blue porcelain bowl
shot to hell.

IMPASSE

You seem to like going to that foul, green-walled place
where every last water fountain is dried up and the only reprieve
is a pool of old-lady spit and a torn paper cup. Stop
taking me there, stop forcing me
up against that stinking wall just so you can tell me again
how little you care for the way I chew my steak.

I hate the way you blow your nose when you've got the flu,
how you leave a trail of wet, knotted Kleenexes on every table
in the house. I hate the way you lounge around in your pyjamas
all morning listening to the stereo. I loathe that
twangy spoon and fiddle.

Music. Ha.

A COUNTRY / UN PAYS

These things I can't explain: why your eyes cloud over
when Vigneault comes on the radio singing
  Il me reste un pays à semer
and why when we hold each other, closer than breath,
it feels we're a time zone apart. After you left
for work, I ran my hand through your wardrobe of shirts,
their collars and sleeves emptied
of your smell.

The first snow of the season
made you wistful, its haunted breath
whispering after you, shadowing you
like a ghost.

You are alone on the couch
listening to your songs; I'm by the small, practical light
of the stove reading your blue dictionary.

Country: *Région, contrée, ville*
où l'on est né, patrie. Avant que d'être à vous
je suis à mon pays.

SOLITAIRE

A paper cup and your dozing head
in the isolate light
of the college stacks.

Rooted in Longfellow's poem
about Gabriel and Evangeline
parted at the Acadian expulsion
in 1755,

fiery lovers
bobbing in your unconscious mind
like the desperate message
corked in a bottle and flung out to sea,

words that will surface again
somewhere on the planet

years from now.

TRUCE

Look closely and you'll find me,
pencilled into the horizon

trying to salvage what's left

of the tangleweed yard,
the last glum tomatoes
in the dwindling light.

Look again, and see yourself
standing at the window,

traces of your breath on the pane
leaving a pale heart.

Granted, it's not much
of an apology
but it's the closest I can get
to the two of us

crouched in the dirt
with our trowels
and a handful of seeds

radiant in the first spring light
across our faces.

COMMUNION

My cashmere sweater is ressurrected
as a housecoat for my son. He wears it after the bath
over his terry sleepers, shapeless turquoise garment
trailing the floor, huge and all sleeves,
doily collar so frail, it'll disintegrate
in the next wash.

When I was a kid, my mother babied it,
packing and unpacking a brown trunk of mothballs,
inspecting the elbows every Sunday for pinhole larvae.
We dressed for church in those days—
girls in wide hats and lace, our passing reflections
in the blond oak pews as we took turns at the chalice
lapping our velvet band of light, holy tonguefuls
of Madonna and child, of Jesus and death

the attic smell of a crucified body
on the eve of decay, like a spotted leaf
absorbing the white, white light
and finally ascending.

EASTER MORNING (AFTER THE ICE STORM)
for Pierre Laporte

The trees are shabby this spring.
A porch swing
creaks in the distance.

They say it will come suddenly
and without warning—a moment
of tremendous clarity and insight
like an unexpected chill
up the spine.

I shiver under the stars, waiting
for the first tinge of light
over the city, palest white
gentling into peach,
peach into lilac

colour settling little by little
over the emptiness.

At dawn, you surround me
like lungfuls of air, your body
redolent of pine, your composted organs
fattening the worms

your soul in each pale shoot of grass
nudging its way up through the soil.

MEMORIAM

for Jean Jacob

1

Huddled under a lamppost after his funeral,
our orphaned mouths are gaping
black holes.

His presence seethes in the shadows—
yeastlike, human, the warm heap of a man
pruning his backyard trees,
their sloshing heads of fruit.

We cling to him
as bare arms cling
to a summer shawl.

Overhead, the gauzy gnats
make their brief appearance

while the sky thickens

vermilion to black,

doubling itself
exponentially.

2

Stars appear out of nowhere, snapping
into their nightly positions.

Every atom, every winking soul is a blip in the cosmos.

For this, we are needy. Stories, a way
to package the abstract.

We sit in the dark, prophetically connecting
the dots—

how, forty years ago, on its maiden voyage
his soft bone head swam up through
a narrow channel and burst into this world
on a shimmering lake of placenta;

how waterlogged he looked after the downpour
when he left his car windows open

squashing around the yard in rubber boots,
blowdryer in one hand, beach pail in the other
trying to flush out the mess;

how he must have looked in his last moments—
bloated digits clawing the hull of his boat,
lungs filling up faster than he could bail them out,

his billowing body at the end of a taut rope,
aimless as seaweed.

These and other watery details an anchor
for the living.

3

I lie awake listening for cars, watching their headlights
throw diamonds across my ceiling.

The tidied household waiting for tomorrow—spotless linens,
bureaus of folded slacks, the coffee-maker
on auto-pilot.

I ponder the deviant planets, the blur of him
at twilight by his cluttered shed.

Our last conversation
through a feathered hedge—
two vague silhouettes
straining to hear each other
above the wind.

The fact that his last muffled words to me
could have been anything, the way
a sealed letter on the credenza
contains every articulation of love or anger,
every epic poem, every imagined
permutation and combination
of language.

Details that didn't make his obituary—
that he studied art in Paris, that his abstract
canvasses spilled over into the ordinary world, that
whenever it rained, a few damp curls
strayed out the front of his hood
and hung in long, messy scribbles
over his eyes.

VISITING RODIN

1. St-Antoine-de-Tilly

Scrawled on the lip of the overpass—
La vie peut nous séparer
and a lopsided heart beside it,
some tortured adolescent risking her life
and the one tube of lipstick she owns
for a boy.

In their village, daisies breeding wildly
by the side of the road,
a handful of houses, the abandoned white church
they will crouch behind, their innocent bodies
flowering in the breeze.

We arrive at the inn just as the sun noses
into the matted horizon.

Order steak and Beaujolais up to the room. Check the TV listings.
Unseal every bathroom glass. Unpack the suitcases.

When we've nothing left to open, we orchestrate
some kind of love in a foreign bed.

2. Driving

Headed for the museum in Quebec City,
an emaciated white cloud over our car.

Gauzy ligaments
barely holding themselves together.

It hounds us for miles of brushcut fields
and hay waiting in dumb yellow spools
like a congregation of penned-in sheep.
You sing along with the radio.
I watch the speedometer, killing time.

Replay last night's lovemaking, accurate
to a fault.

Whereas Rodin was always inventing
new forms, new ways for man to connect.

Even if it meant altering the details
of anatomy—enlarging a head,
subtracting a penis.

We drive by bony things
that pass for trees,

their grey, contorted branches
snapped at the neck.

3. The Large Shade

You stop to relieve yourself by the side of the road,
pawing through the bramble
like an animal
staking its territory.

With each passing moment, another car and
I am embarrassed for both of us, until

a sudden cloud obstructs the sun,
darkness crossing the field
like a curtain

casting you momentarily
in a softer light,

strained cord of your neck
slackening some, a gentle relief
of muscles through your shirt—

perfect marriage
of plane and shadow.

4. The Kiss

Hands floured in plaster, Rodin spoke
in depths rather than surfaces.
Sculpted what was seething beneath the skin
rather than a mere body part.

Not just an ordinary wrist
but the raised, blue rivering of veins
or the rough-hewn interior of a mouth
gasping for air.

Inevitably, we are drawn to Dante's lovers
looped through one another and
drenched in light, like a couple
of gleaming seals washed ashore.

Francesca da Rimini and Paolo Malatesta
moments before her jealous husband
discovers their crime
and murders them—

the solid, ringed muscle of his chest,
their joined feet,
the huge floodgates in her body
about to let go.

Subconsciously, I reach for your hand,
a salt-line of dew along my forehead.

Nipples drifting like pond lilies
under my blouse.

We gaze at the bronze all morning it seems,

speechless, overwhelmed,
heads hung in shock
and in awe.

IN A PERFECT WORLD

In the orchard at dawn
our heads brush the pendant trees

arterial and intimately
connected.

Gradually, my heart unclenches
and I begin to see

sky and field
as parts of the same whole

one blue, one green
but barely distinguishable.

We meet at the blurred juncture—

russet fruit mellowing in the light, silhouettes
of you and me on a tall fence

leaves and apple boughs
breezing through our hair.

TENTATIVE

à un poète québécois,
Trois-Rivières, 1996

1

ce n'est pas ta maladie qui nous sépare
mais le virus du quotidien, le sang froid
d'octobre

voici l'heure sombre du départ

je te quitte, je ne te verrai plus
tout le monde sait
qu'un orage défait le ciel

peut-être un jour me rappelerais-je
une gorgée de vin, un simple partage
au bistro

et les tristes vers
de ta jeunesse

2

tu vas mourir, on le voit
dans la vaste noirceur envahissant
tes yeux, l'humble vouloir
de s'accrocher à la vie
à tout ce qui tremble
au vent

au bref moment de soleil
qui touche à ta peau
et t'éclaircit

3

ta blessure s'aggrave
j'ai peur de t'toucher

le corps est une sorte de prison

je m'étends sous le pommier
avec mon carnet
et le parfum
de la terre

il s'agit de le dire
tout simplement

il ne faut pas se taire

"ce qui mange ton sang
ne mangera jamais ton âme"

la nuit avance
et je commence
à peine

d'écrire

NOTES

ARGUMENT
J'en ai assez vu: I've seen enough
Y existe pas, Dieu: God doesn't exist

LAST THOUGHTS OF PIERRE LAPORTE
Domtar: a large pulp and paper mill housed in Windsor, Quebec about 130
    kilometres east of Montreal.

MON ONCLE RICHARD
réveillon: custom of staying up late into the night on Christmas Eve
tourtière: a traditional meat pie
crisse de ciment: goddam cement
crisse de Noël: goddam Christmas

LA GROSSE MAUDITE ANGLAISE (BIG, FAT, DAMNED ENGLISH LADY)
On est fait comme des rats: We're in deep trouble
le gouvernement est une maudite grosse machine: the government is a goddam huge machine

ORPHAN
joual: a Québécois dialect
poutine: a fast-food specialty: French fries smothered in gravy with a curd cheese topping
quétaine: tacky, cheap-looking

THE OLD DAYS
Comme ta p'tite soeur à toé, ou la mienne: Like your little sister or mine

REFERENDUM DAY IN CHARLEVOIX
les bons vivants: happy-go-lucky types, pleasure-seekers

SUNDAY DRIVE
Maudite bonne idée. En même temps on ira voir les légumes au parlement:
    Damn good idea. While we're at it, we'll go visit the vegetables in Parliament.

A COUNTRY / UN PAYS

Il me reste un pays à semer: I still have a country to seed
Région, contrée, ville où l'on est né, patrie: Place of birth, homeland
Avant que d'être à vous je suis à mon pays:

> Before giving myself to you, I give myself to my country.

According to the dictionary, the quotation is from French dramatist Pierre Corneille
(1606-1684).

VISITING RODIN

La vie peut nous séparer: Life can tear us apart

TENTATIVE (ATTEMPT)

to a Quebec poet
Trois-Rivières, 1996

1
it's not your illness that separates us
but the virus of routine, the cold blood
of October

it is upon us—the grey hour of departure

I am leaving you for good
everyone knows
that a storm's undoing the sky

perhaps one day I'll recall
a sip of wine, a simple meal
at the restaurant

and the depressing tunes
of your childhood

2
you're going to die, we can see it
in the huge darkness invading
your eyes, the humble need

to latch onto life
onto everything trembling
in the wind

onto the brief glimmer of sun
that touches your skin
and illumines you

3
your wound is widening
I'm afraid to touch you

the body is a kind of prison

I lie under the apple tree
with my notebook
and the perfumed
earth

one must say it
simply

one must not remain silent

"that which devours your blood
will never devour your soul"

night is falling
and I have
barely begun

to write

Printed in October 1999 by

in Longueuil, Quebec